50 Premium Casserole Recipes for Cozy Nights

By: Kelly Johnson

Table of Contents

- Classic Chicken and Rice Casserole
- Beef and Cheese Lasagna
- Creamy Tuna Noodle Casserole
- Broccoli Cheddar Chicken Casserole
- Beef Stroganoff Casserole
- Baked Ziti with Sausage
- Sweet Potato and Sausage Casserole
- Chicken Alfredo Casserole
- Mexican Taco Casserole
- Baked Macaroni and Cheese
- Shepherd's Pie with Garlic Mashed Potatoes
- Spinach and Artichoke Dip Casserole
- Chicken Parmesan Casserole
- Sausage and Pepper Frittata
- Shrimp and Grits Casserole
- Ham and Cheese Breakfast Casserole
- Sweet Potato and Black Bean Casserole
- Pulled Pork and Cornbread Casserole
- Baked Eggplant Parmesan
- Chicken Enchilada Casserole
- Creamy Broccoli and Rice Casserole
- Turkey and Stuffing Casserole
- Spinach and Ricotta Lasagna
- BBQ Chicken Casserole
- Baked Gnocchi with Tomato and Mozzarella
- Beef and Mushroom Casserole
- Zucchini and Ground Turkey Casserole
- Ham, Potato, and Broccoli Casserole
- Beef and Sweet Potato Shepherd's Pie
- Chicken, Bacon, and Ranch Casserole
- Philly Cheesesteak Casserole
- Crab Mac and Cheese
- Chicken and Dumplings Casserole
- Beef and Bean Chili Casserole
- Veggie-Stuffed Quinoa Casserole

- Shrimp Scampi Casserole
- Chicken and Pesto Pasta Bake
- Classic Scalloped Potatoes
- Ratatouille Casserole
- Sausage and Spinach Stuffed Shells
- Meatball Sub Casserole
- Greek Chicken and Rice Casserole
- Cheesy Potato and Bacon Casserole
- Buffalo Chicken Casserole
- Lemon and Herb Chicken Casserole
- Baked Spaghetti Carbonara
- Cranberry and Walnut Stuffing Casserole
- Roasted Cauliflower and Cheese Casserole
- Beef and Potato Hash Casserole
- Chicken and Bacon Ranch Pasta Casserole

Classic Chicken and Rice Casserole

Ingredients:

- **2 cups cooked chicken**, shredded
- **1 1/2 cups rice** (uncooked)
- **1 can cream of chicken soup**
- **1 can diced tomatoes** (optional)
- **2 cups chicken broth**
- **1 onion**, chopped
- **1 cup frozen peas**
- **1/2 cup shredded cheddar cheese**
- **1/2 cup milk**
- **Salt and pepper**, to taste

Instructions:

1. Preheat the oven to 350°F (175°C).
2. In a large casserole dish, combine the rice, cream of chicken soup, chicken broth, diced tomatoes (if using), onion, peas, and shredded chicken. Mix well.
3. Pour in the milk and stir everything together. Season with salt and pepper.
4. Cover the casserole with aluminum foil and bake for 40-45 minutes.
5. Remove the foil and sprinkle with cheddar cheese. Bake for an additional 5-10 minutes, until the cheese is melted and bubbly.
6. Serve hot.

Beef and Cheese Lasagna

Ingredients:

- **1 lb ground beef**
- **1 onion**, chopped
- **2 cloves garlic**, minced
- **1 jar marinara sauce**
- **1 package lasagna noodles** (cooked and drained)
- **1 1/2 cups ricotta cheese**
- **2 cups shredded mozzarella cheese**
- **1/2 cup grated Parmesan cheese**
- **1 egg**, beaten
- **1 tablespoon Italian seasoning**
- **Salt and pepper**, to taste

Instructions:

1. Preheat the oven to 375°F (190°C).
2. In a large skillet, cook the ground beef with chopped onion and garlic until browned. Drain excess fat. Add marinara sauce, Italian seasoning, salt, and pepper. Simmer for 10 minutes.
3. In a separate bowl, combine ricotta cheese, beaten egg, and 1/2 cup of mozzarella cheese. Mix well.
4. In a baking dish, spread a thin layer of meat sauce. Layer cooked lasagna noodles, followed by ricotta mixture, meat sauce, and mozzarella cheese. Repeat layers until ingredients are used.
5. Finish with a top layer of meat sauce and the remaining mozzarella and Parmesan cheeses.
6. Cover with foil and bake for 25 minutes. Remove foil and bake for an additional 10-15 minutes, until bubbly and golden.
7. Let the lasagna rest for 10 minutes before serving.

Creamy Tuna Noodle Casserole

Ingredients:

- 2 cans tuna in water, drained
- 2 cups egg noodles, cooked and drained
- 1 can cream of mushroom soup
- 1/2 cup milk
- 1/2 cup frozen peas
- 1/2 cup shredded cheddar cheese
- 1/2 cup breadcrumbs
- 1 tablespoon butter, melted
- 1/2 teaspoon garlic powder
- Salt and pepper, to taste

Instructions:

1. Preheat the oven to 350°F (175°C).
2. In a large bowl, combine the cooked egg noodles, drained tuna, cream of mushroom soup, milk, peas, garlic powder, salt, and pepper. Mix well.
3. Transfer the mixture to a greased casserole dish. Top with shredded cheddar cheese.
4. In a small bowl, combine the melted butter and breadcrumbs. Sprinkle the breadcrumb mixture over the cheese.
5. Bake for 20-25 minutes, until the casserole is bubbly and the breadcrumbs are golden.
6. Serve hot.

Broccoli Cheddar Chicken Casserole

Ingredients:

- **2 cups cooked chicken**, shredded
- **2 cups broccoli florets**, steamed
- **1 can cream of chicken soup**
- **1/2 cup sour cream**
- **2 cups shredded cheddar cheese**
- **1/2 cup cooked rice** (optional)
- **1/2 cup breadcrumbs** (optional for topping)
- **Salt and pepper**, to taste

Instructions:

1. Preheat the oven to 350°F (175°C).
2. In a large mixing bowl, combine the cooked chicken, steamed broccoli, cream of chicken soup, sour cream, cooked rice (if using), and 1 cup of cheddar cheese. Season with salt and pepper.
3. Pour the mixture into a greased casserole dish and top with the remaining cheddar cheese.
4. If desired, sprinkle breadcrumbs on top for extra crunch.
5. Bake for 20-25 minutes, until bubbly and the cheese is melted.
6. Serve hot.

Beef Stroganoff Casserole

Ingredients:

- 1 lb ground beef
- 1 onion, chopped
- 1 can cream of mushroom soup
- 1/2 cup sour cream
- 2 cups cooked egg noodles
- 1/2 cup shredded cheddar cheese
- 1 tablespoon Worcestershire sauce
- 1 teaspoon garlic powder
- **Salt and pepper**, to taste

Instructions:

1. Preheat the oven to 350°F (175°C).
2. In a skillet, cook the ground beef with the chopped onion until browned. Drain excess fat.
3. Stir in the cream of mushroom soup, sour cream, Worcestershire sauce, garlic powder, salt, and pepper. Let the mixture simmer for 5 minutes.
4. Add the cooked egg noodles to the beef mixture and stir to combine.
5. Transfer everything to a greased casserole dish and top with shredded cheddar cheese.
6. Bake for 20-25 minutes, until bubbly and golden.
7. Serve hot.

Baked Ziti with Sausage

Ingredients:

- **1 lb Italian sausage**, crumbled
- **1 jar marinara sauce**
- **1 lb ziti pasta**, cooked and drained
- **1 1/2 cups ricotta cheese**
- **2 cups shredded mozzarella cheese**
- **1/2 cup grated Parmesan cheese**
- **1 tablespoon Italian seasoning**
- **Salt and pepper**, to taste

Instructions:

1. Preheat the oven to 375°F (190°C).
2. In a large skillet, cook the sausage until browned. Drain any excess fat and stir in marinara sauce. Simmer for 5 minutes.
3. In a large bowl, combine the cooked ziti, ricotta cheese, mozzarella cheese, Parmesan cheese, and Italian seasoning. Mix well.
4. Add the sausage mixture to the pasta and stir to combine.
5. Transfer the mixture to a greased baking dish and top with additional mozzarella cheese.
6. Bake for 25-30 minutes, until bubbly and golden.
7. Serve hot.

Sweet Potato and Sausage Casserole

Ingredients:

- **2 large sweet potatoes**, peeled and cubed
- **1 lb sausage**, crumbled
- **1 onion**, chopped
- **1 cup chicken broth**
- **1/2 teaspoon cinnamon**
- **1/2 teaspoon paprika**
- **Salt and pepper**, to taste

Instructions:

1. Preheat the oven to 375°F (190°C).
2. In a skillet, cook the sausage and onion until browned. Remove from heat.
3. In a large bowl, combine the cubed sweet potatoes, sausage mixture, chicken broth, cinnamon, paprika, salt, and pepper.
4. Transfer everything to a greased casserole dish and cover with foil.
5. Bake for 35-40 minutes, until the sweet potatoes are tender.
6. Serve hot.

Chicken Alfredo Casserole

Ingredients:

- 2 cups cooked chicken, shredded
- 1 lb cooked penne pasta
- 1 jar Alfredo sauce
- 1 cup shredded mozzarella cheese
- 1/2 cup grated Parmesan cheese
- 1/4 cup breadcrumbs (optional for topping)
- Salt and pepper, to taste

Instructions:

1. Preheat the oven to 350°F (175°C).
2. In a large bowl, combine the cooked chicken, cooked pasta, Alfredo sauce, mozzarella cheese, and Parmesan cheese. Season with salt and pepper.
3. Transfer the mixture to a greased casserole dish and top with additional mozzarella cheese.
4. If desired, sprinkle breadcrumbs on top for extra crunch.
5. Bake for 20-25 minutes, until bubbly and golden.
6. Serve hot.

Mexican Taco Casserole

Ingredients:

- 1 lb ground beef
- 1 packet taco seasoning
- **1 can black beans**, drained and rinsed
- 1 cup corn kernels
- 1 cup shredded cheddar cheese
- 1 cup salsa
- **Tortilla chips**, crushed
- **Sour cream** (for serving)
- **Chopped green onions** (for garnish)

Instructions:

1. Preheat the oven to 350°F (175°C).
2. In a skillet, cook the ground beef until browned. Drain excess fat and stir in taco seasoning. Add the black beans and corn, and cook for an additional 3 minutes.
3. In a casserole dish, layer the beef mixture, crushed tortilla chips, salsa, and shredded cheddar cheese.
4. Bake for 20 minutes, until the cheese is melted and bubbly.
5. Top with sour cream and chopped green onions before serving.

Baked Macaroni and Cheese

Ingredients:

- **1 lb elbow macaroni**, cooked and drained
- **4 cups shredded sharp cheddar cheese**
- **2 cups milk**
- **1/2 cup heavy cream**
- **1/4 cup butter**
- **1/4 cup all-purpose flour**
- **1 teaspoon garlic powder**
- **1 teaspoon mustard powder**
- **Salt and pepper**, to taste
- **1 cup breadcrumbs** (optional topping)

Instructions:

1. Preheat the oven to 350°F (175°C).
2. In a large pot, melt butter over medium heat. Whisk in flour, garlic powder, mustard powder, salt, and pepper. Cook for 2 minutes.
3. Gradually add milk and cream, whisking constantly until the sauce thickens.
4. Stir in 3 cups of cheddar cheese and mix until melted and smooth.
5. Add the cooked macaroni to the cheese sauce and stir to coat.
6. Transfer to a greased baking dish. Top with remaining cheddar cheese and breadcrumbs.
7. Bake for 20-25 minutes, until bubbly and golden.
8. Serve hot.

Shepherd's Pie with Garlic Mashed Potatoes

Ingredients:

- **1 lb ground beef or lamb**
- **1 onion**, chopped
- **2 cloves garlic**, minced
- **1 cup frozen peas**
- **2 carrots**, diced
- **1/4 cup beef broth**
- **1 tablespoon tomato paste**
- **2 cups garlic mashed potatoes**
- **Salt and pepper**, to taste

Instructions:

1. Preheat the oven to 375°F (190°C).
2. In a skillet, cook the ground meat with onion and garlic until browned. Drain excess fat.
3. Add diced carrots, peas, beef broth, and tomato paste to the skillet. Simmer for 5 minutes.
4. Season with salt and pepper, then transfer the mixture to a greased casserole dish.
5. Spread the garlic mashed potatoes over the meat mixture, smoothing it into an even layer.
6. Bake for 20-25 minutes, until the top is golden and crispy.
7. Serve hot.

Spinach and Artichoke Dip Casserole

Ingredients:

- **1 can artichoke hearts**, drained and chopped
- **1 package frozen spinach**, thawed and drained
- **1/2 cup sour cream**
- **1/2 cup mayonnaise**
- **1 cup grated Parmesan cheese**
- **1 cup shredded mozzarella cheese**
- **1 clove garlic**, minced
- **1/2 teaspoon garlic powder**
- **Salt and pepper**, to taste

Instructions:

1. Preheat the oven to 350°F (175°C).
2. In a bowl, combine chopped artichokes, spinach, sour cream, mayonnaise, Parmesan cheese, mozzarella cheese, garlic, garlic powder, salt, and pepper. Mix well.
3. Transfer the mixture to a greased casserole dish.
4. Bake for 20-25 minutes, until the top is golden and bubbly.
5. Serve warm with crackers or bread.

Chicken Parmesan Casserole

Ingredients:

- **2 cups cooked chicken**, shredded
- **1 jar marinara sauce**
- **1 package cooked penne pasta**
- **1 cup shredded mozzarella cheese**
- **1/2 cup grated Parmesan cheese**
- **1 teaspoon Italian seasoning**
- **Salt and pepper**, to taste

Instructions:

1. Preheat the oven to 375°F (190°C).
2. In a large bowl, combine the cooked chicken, marinara sauce, cooked pasta, mozzarella cheese, and Parmesan cheese.
3. Season with Italian seasoning, salt, and pepper.
4. Transfer to a greased casserole dish and top with additional mozzarella and Parmesan cheese.
5. Bake for 20-25 minutes, until bubbly and golden.
6. Serve hot.

Sausage and Pepper Frittata

Ingredients:

- **1 lb Italian sausage**, crumbled
- **1 bell pepper**, diced
- **1 onion**, diced
- **10 large eggs**
- **1/2 cup milk**
- **1 cup shredded mozzarella cheese**
- **Salt and pepper**, to taste

Instructions:

1. Preheat the oven to 375°F (190°C).
2. In a skillet, cook the sausage, bell pepper, and onion until browned. Drain excess fat.
3. In a bowl, whisk together eggs, milk, salt, and pepper.
4. Pour the egg mixture over the sausage and pepper mixture in the skillet. Stir gently.
5. Sprinkle shredded mozzarella cheese over the top.
6. Transfer the skillet to the oven and bake for 15-20 minutes, until the eggs are set and the top is golden.
7. Serve hot.

Shrimp and Grits Casserole

Ingredients:

- 1 lb shrimp, peeled and deveined
- 2 cups cooked grits
- 1/2 cup shredded cheddar cheese
- 1/4 cup cream cheese
- 1/2 cup milk
- 1/4 cup butter
- 1 tablespoon Cajun seasoning
- 1/2 cup green onions, chopped
- Salt and pepper, to taste

Instructions:

1. Preheat the oven to 350°F (175°C).
2. In a skillet, cook the shrimp with Cajun seasoning until pink and cooked through. Set aside.
3. In a separate saucepan, combine cooked grits, cream cheese, milk, butter, and shredded cheddar cheese. Stir until smooth.
4. In a greased casserole dish, layer the grits mixture, shrimp, and green onions.
5. Bake for 15-20 minutes, until bubbly.
6. Serve hot.

Ham and Cheese Breakfast Casserole

Ingredients:

- 2 cups diced ham
- 1 cup shredded cheddar cheese
- 8 large eggs
- 1 cup milk
- 1/2 cup diced onion
- 1/2 cup bell pepper, diced
- 1/2 teaspoon garlic powder
- Salt and pepper, to taste

Instructions:

1. Preheat the oven to 350°F (175°C).
2. In a large bowl, whisk together eggs, milk, garlic powder, salt, and pepper.
3. In a greased casserole dish, layer diced ham, shredded cheddar cheese, onion, and bell pepper.
4. Pour the egg mixture over the top and stir gently to combine.
5. Bake for 25-30 minutes, until the eggs are set and golden.
6. Serve hot.

Sweet Potato and Black Bean Casserole

Ingredients:

- **2 large sweet potatoes**, peeled and cubed
- **1 can black beans**, drained and rinsed
- **1/2 cup salsa**
- **1 cup shredded cheddar cheese**
- **1 teaspoon cumin**
- **1/2 teaspoon chili powder**
- **Salt and pepper**, to taste

Instructions:

1. Preheat the oven to 375°F (190°C).
2. In a large bowl, combine cubed sweet potatoes, black beans, salsa, cumin, chili powder, salt, and pepper.
3. Transfer to a greased casserole dish and top with shredded cheddar cheese.
4. Bake for 30-35 minutes, until the sweet potatoes are tender and the cheese is melted.
5. Serve hot.

Pulled Pork and Cornbread Casserole

Ingredients:

- **2 cups pulled pork**, cooked
- **1 box cornbread mix**, prepared according to package instructions
- **1 cup barbecue sauce**
- **1 cup shredded cheddar cheese**
- **1/2 cup green onions**, chopped

Instructions:

1. Preheat the oven to 350°F (175°C).
2. In a bowl, mix pulled pork with barbecue sauce.
3. Spread the pulled pork mixture into a greased casserole dish.
4. Pour the prepared cornbread batter over the pork mixture and spread evenly.
5. Top with shredded cheddar cheese.
6. Bake for 25-30 minutes, until the cornbread is golden and cooked through.
7. Garnish with chopped green onions before serving.

Baked Eggplant Parmesan

Ingredients:

- **2 large eggplants**, sliced into 1/2-inch thick rounds
- **1 cup breadcrumbs**
- **1/2 cup grated Parmesan cheese**
- **2 cups marinara sauce**
- **2 cups shredded mozzarella cheese**
- **2 eggs**, beaten
- **1 teaspoon dried basil**
- **1 teaspoon dried oregano**
- **Olive oil**, for drizzling
- **Salt and pepper**, to taste

Instructions:

1. Preheat the oven to 375°F (190°C).
2. In a shallow dish, mix breadcrumbs, Parmesan, basil, and oregano.
3. Dip each eggplant slice into the beaten eggs, then coat with the breadcrumb mixture.
4. Arrange the eggplant slices on a baking sheet, drizzle with olive oil, and bake for 20 minutes, flipping halfway through.
5. In a greased casserole dish, spread a layer of marinara sauce, then add a layer of baked eggplant slices. Top with mozzarella cheese.
6. Repeat the layers until all eggplant is used.
7. Bake for an additional 15-20 minutes, until the cheese is melted and bubbly.
8. Serve hot.

Chicken Enchilada Casserole

Ingredients:

- **2 cups cooked chicken**, shredded
- **1 can red enchilada sauce**
- **1 can diced green chilies**
- **1 cup corn kernels**
- **1 cup black beans**, drained and rinsed
- **2 cups shredded cheddar cheese**
- **1 cup sour cream**
- **1 cup chopped green onions**
- **12 corn tortillas**, cut into strips
- **1 teaspoon cumin**
- **1 teaspoon chili powder**
- **Salt and pepper**, to taste

Instructions:

1. Preheat the oven to 350°F (175°C).
2. In a large bowl, mix the shredded chicken, enchilada sauce, diced chilies, corn, black beans, sour cream, green onions, cumin, chili powder, salt, and pepper.
3. Lightly grease a casserole dish and spread a layer of tortilla strips at the bottom.
4. Top with a layer of the chicken mixture and then a sprinkle of shredded cheddar cheese.
5. Repeat the layers until all ingredients are used, finishing with a layer of cheese on top.
6. Bake for 25-30 minutes, until bubbly and golden.
7. Serve hot.

Creamy Broccoli and Rice Casserole

Ingredients:

- 1 cup cooked rice
- 2 cups broccoli florets, steamed
- 1 can cream of mushroom soup
- 1/2 cup sour cream
- 1/2 cup shredded cheddar cheese
- 1/2 cup milk
- 1/4 teaspoon garlic powder
- **Salt and pepper**, to taste
- **1/4 cup breadcrumbs**, optional topping

Instructions:

1. Preheat the oven to 350°F (175°C).
2. In a large bowl, combine cooked rice, steamed broccoli, cream of mushroom soup, sour cream, shredded cheddar cheese, milk, garlic powder, salt, and pepper.
3. Transfer the mixture to a greased casserole dish and spread evenly.
4. If desired, top with breadcrumbs for added texture.
5. Bake for 20-25 minutes, until the top is golden and bubbly.
6. Serve hot.

Turkey and Stuffing Casserole

Ingredients:

- **2 cups cooked turkey**, shredded
- **1 package stuffing mix**
- **1 can cream of chicken soup**
- **1/2 cup chicken broth**
- **1/2 cup sour cream**
- **1/2 cup shredded cheddar cheese**
- **1/2 teaspoon sage**
- **Salt and pepper**, to taste

Instructions:

1. Preheat the oven to 350°F (175°C).
2. In a large bowl, combine the cooked turkey, stuffing mix, cream of chicken soup, chicken broth, sour cream, sage, salt, and pepper.
3. Transfer to a greased casserole dish and top with shredded cheddar cheese.
4. Bake for 20-25 minutes, until golden and bubbly.
5. Serve hot.

Spinach and Ricotta Lasagna

Ingredients:

- **9 lasagna noodles**, cooked and drained
- **1 cup ricotta cheese**
- **2 cups shredded mozzarella cheese**
- **1/2 cup grated Parmesan cheese**
- **2 cups spinach**, wilted and chopped
- **2 cups marinara sauce**
- **1 egg**, beaten
- **1 teaspoon dried oregano**
- **Salt and pepper**, to taste

Instructions:

1. Preheat the oven to 375°F (190°C).
2. In a bowl, mix ricotta cheese, egg, spinach, Parmesan, oregano, salt, and pepper.
3. In a greased casserole dish, spread a layer of marinara sauce. Layer 3 lasagna noodles on top.
4. Spread a layer of the ricotta mixture, then a layer of shredded mozzarella. Repeat the layers two more times.
5. Top with remaining mozzarella cheese and a little more marinara sauce.
6. Cover with foil and bake for 25-30 minutes, then remove the foil and bake for an additional 10 minutes until bubbly and golden.
7. Serve hot.

BBQ Chicken Casserole

Ingredients:

- **2 cups cooked chicken**, shredded
- **1 cup BBQ sauce**
- **1 cup frozen corn**
- **1 cup black beans**, drained and rinsed
- **1 cup shredded cheddar cheese**
- **1/2 cup red onion**, diced
- **1 cup crushed tortilla chips**
- **Salt and pepper**, to taste

Instructions:

1. Preheat the oven to 350°F (175°C).
2. In a large bowl, combine the shredded chicken, BBQ sauce, corn, black beans, red onion, and salt and pepper.
3. Transfer to a greased casserole dish and top with shredded cheddar cheese.
4. Sprinkle crushed tortilla chips on top.
5. Bake for 20-25 minutes, until the cheese is melted and bubbly.
6. Serve hot.

Baked Gnocchi with Tomato and Mozzarella

Ingredients:

- 1 lb gnocchi
- 2 cups marinara sauce
- 2 cups shredded mozzarella cheese
- 1/2 cup grated Parmesan cheese
- 1 teaspoon dried basil
- **Salt and pepper**, to taste

Instructions:

1. Preheat the oven to 375°F (190°C).
2. Cook the gnocchi according to package instructions and drain.
3. In a large bowl, toss the gnocchi with marinara sauce, mozzarella cheese, Parmesan, basil, salt, and pepper.
4. Transfer to a greased casserole dish and top with additional mozzarella cheese.
5. Bake for 20-25 minutes, until the top is golden and bubbly.
6. Serve hot.

Beef and Mushroom Casserole

Ingredients:

- **1 lb ground beef**
- **1 onion**, diced
- **1 cup mushrooms**, sliced
- **1 can cream of mushroom soup**
- **1/2 cup beef broth**
- **1 cup cooked rice**
- **1 cup shredded cheddar cheese**
- **Salt and pepper**, to taste

Instructions:

1. Preheat the oven to 350°F (175°C).
2. In a skillet, cook the ground beef and diced onion until browned. Drain excess fat.
3. Add sliced mushrooms and cook for an additional 5 minutes.
4. Stir in cream of mushroom soup, beef broth, cooked rice, salt, and pepper.
5. Transfer to a greased casserole dish and top with shredded cheddar cheese.
6. Bake for 20-25 minutes, until bubbly and golden.
7. Serve hot.

Zucchini and Ground Turkey Casserole

Ingredients:

- **2 medium zucchinis**, sliced
- **1 lb ground turkey**
- **1 onion**, diced
- **1 can diced tomatoes**
- **1/2 cup shredded mozzarella cheese**
- **1 teaspoon Italian seasoning**
- **Salt and pepper**, to taste

Instructions:

1. Preheat the oven to 350°F (175°C).
2. In a skillet, cook the ground turkey and diced onion until browned. Drain excess fat.
3. Add the sliced zucchini, diced tomatoes, Italian seasoning, salt, and pepper. Cook for 5 minutes, until zucchini is tender.
4. Transfer the mixture to a greased casserole dish and top with shredded mozzarella cheese.
5. Bake for 20-25 minutes, until the cheese is melted and bubbly.
6. Serve hot.

Ham, Potato, and Broccoli Casserole

Ingredients:

- **2 cups cooked ham**, diced
- **4 medium potatoes**, peeled and diced
- **2 cups broccoli florets**, steamed
- **1 can cream of mushroom soup**
- **1/2 cup sour cream**
- **1 cup shredded cheddar cheese**
- **1/2 cup milk**
- **1 teaspoon garlic powder**
- **Salt and pepper**, to taste
- **1/2 cup breadcrumbs**, optional topping

Instructions:

1. Preheat the oven to 350°F (175°C).
2. In a large bowl, combine diced ham, potatoes, steamed broccoli, cream of mushroom soup, sour cream, shredded cheddar, milk, garlic powder, salt, and pepper.
3. Transfer to a greased casserole dish and top with breadcrumbs if desired.
4. Bake for 35-40 minutes, until the potatoes are tender and the top is golden.
5. Serve hot.

Beef and Sweet Potato Shepherd's Pie

Ingredients:

- **1 lb ground beef**
- **2 medium sweet potatoes**, peeled and cubed
- **1 small onion**, diced
- **1 cup frozen peas and carrots**
- **1/2 cup beef broth**
- **2 tablespoons tomato paste**
- **1 tablespoon Worcestershire sauce**
- **1/2 teaspoon dried thyme**
- **1/2 teaspoon garlic powder**
- **1/4 cup butter**
- **Salt and pepper**, to taste

Instructions:

1. Preheat the oven to 375°F (190°C).
2. Boil the sweet potatoes in salted water until tender, about 15 minutes. Drain and mash with butter, garlic powder, salt, and pepper.
3. In a skillet, cook the ground beef and diced onion until browned. Add peas, carrots, beef broth, tomato paste, Worcestershire sauce, thyme, salt, and pepper. Simmer for 5-7 minutes.
4. Transfer the beef mixture to a greased casserole dish and top with the mashed sweet potatoes.
5. Bake for 20-25 minutes, until the top is golden and bubbly.
6. Serve hot.

Chicken, Bacon, and Ranch Casserole

Ingredients:

- **2 cups cooked chicken**, shredded
- **6 slices bacon**, cooked and crumbled
- **1 packet ranch seasoning mix**
- **1 cup sour cream**
- **1 cup shredded cheddar cheese**
- **1 cup cooked pasta**
- **1/2 cup chicken broth**
- **1/2 cup green onions**, chopped
- **Salt and pepper**, to taste

Instructions:

1. Preheat the oven to 350°F (175°C).
2. In a large bowl, combine shredded chicken, crumbled bacon, ranch seasoning, sour cream, cheddar cheese, cooked pasta, chicken broth, green onions, salt, and pepper.
3. Transfer to a greased casserole dish and spread evenly.
4. Bake for 20-25 minutes, until the cheese is melted and bubbly.
5. Serve hot.

Philly Cheesesteak Casserole

Ingredients:

- **1 lb beef steak**, thinly sliced (rib-eye or flank steak)
- **1 onion**, diced
- **1 bell pepper**, diced
- **1 cup shredded provolone cheese**
- **1 cup shredded cheddar cheese**
- **1/2 cup mayonnaise**
- **1 tablespoon Dijon mustard**
- **1 teaspoon garlic powder**
- **1 tablespoon olive oil**
- **1 cup cooked pasta**
- **Salt and pepper**, to taste

Instructions:

1. Preheat the oven to 350°F (175°C).
2. In a skillet, cook the beef steak with olive oil until browned. Remove from the pan and set aside.
3. In the same skillet, cook the diced onion and bell pepper until softened, about 5 minutes.
4. In a large bowl, mix together the beef, onion, bell pepper, shredded cheeses, mayonnaise, mustard, garlic powder, cooked pasta, salt, and pepper.
5. Transfer the mixture to a greased casserole dish and bake for 20-25 minutes, until bubbly.
6. Serve hot.

Crab Mac and Cheese

Ingredients:

- 2 cups cooked elbow macaroni
- 1/2 lb lump crab meat
- 2 cups shredded cheddar cheese
- 1 cup shredded mozzarella cheese
- 2 tablespoons butter
- 2 tablespoons flour
- 2 cups milk
- 1 teaspoon garlic powder
- 1 teaspoon Old Bay seasoning
- **Salt and pepper**, to taste

Instructions:

1. Preheat the oven to 350°F (175°C).
2. In a large pot, melt butter over medium heat. Stir in flour and cook for 1-2 minutes.
3. Gradually add milk, whisking constantly until the sauce thickens. Stir in the cheddar and mozzarella cheese, garlic powder, Old Bay, salt, and pepper.
4. Stir in the cooked macaroni and crab meat.
5. Transfer to a greased casserole dish and bake for 20-25 minutes, until bubbly.
6. Serve hot.

Chicken and Dumplings Casserole

Ingredients:

- 2 cups cooked chicken, shredded
- 1 can cream of chicken soup
- 1/2 cup chicken broth
- 1 cup frozen mixed vegetables
- 1 cup shredded cheddar cheese
- 1 package biscuit dough
- 1/2 teaspoon garlic powder
- **Salt and pepper**, to taste

Instructions:

1. Preheat the oven to 350°F (175°C).
2. In a large bowl, combine the cooked chicken, cream of chicken soup, chicken broth, mixed vegetables, shredded cheese, garlic powder, salt, and pepper.
3. Transfer to a greased casserole dish.
4. Tear the biscuit dough into pieces and scatter on top of the casserole.
5. Bake for 25-30 minutes, until the biscuits are golden brown and the casserole is bubbly.
6. Serve hot.

Beef and Bean Chili Casserole

Ingredients:

- **1 lb ground beef**
- **1 can kidney beans**, drained and rinsed
- **1 can black beans**, drained and rinsed
- **1 can diced tomatoes**
- **1 packet chili seasoning mix**
- **1 cup shredded cheddar cheese**
- **1/2 cup sour cream**
- **1/2 cup green onions**, chopped
- **Salt and pepper**, to taste

Instructions:

1. Preheat the oven to 350°F (175°C).
2. In a skillet, cook the ground beef until browned, then drain excess fat.
3. Add beans, diced tomatoes, chili seasoning, salt, and pepper to the beef. Simmer for 10 minutes.
4. Transfer the mixture to a greased casserole dish and top with shredded cheddar cheese.
5. Bake for 20-25 minutes, until the cheese is melted and bubbly.
6. Serve with sour cream and green onions on top.

Veggie-Stuffed Quinoa Casserole

Ingredients:

- 1 cup cooked quinoa
- 1 cup zucchini, diced
- 1 cup bell peppers, diced
- 1/2 cup red onion, diced
- 1 can diced tomatoes
- 1 cup shredded mozzarella cheese
- 1 teaspoon garlic powder
- 1 teaspoon dried oregano
- Salt and pepper, to taste

Instructions:

1. Preheat the oven to 375°F (190°C).
2. In a skillet, sauté zucchini, bell peppers, and onion until softened.
3. In a large bowl, combine cooked quinoa, sautéed veggies, diced tomatoes, mozzarella cheese, garlic powder, oregano, salt, and pepper.
4. Transfer to a greased casserole dish and bake for 20-25 minutes, until the cheese is melted and bubbly.
5. Serve hot.

Shrimp Scampi Casserole

Ingredients:

- **1 lb shrimp**, peeled and deveined
- **2 cups cooked pasta**
- **3 cloves garlic**, minced
- **1/2 cup butter**
- **1/2 cup white wine**
- **1/2 cup grated Parmesan cheese**
- **1 tablespoon lemon juice**
- **1/4 teaspoon red pepper flakes**
- **1/4 cup fresh parsley**, chopped
- **Salt and pepper**, to taste

Instructions:

1. Preheat the oven to 350°F (175°C).
2. In a skillet, melt butter over medium heat. Add garlic and cook for 1 minute.
3. Add shrimp and cook until pink. Remove shrimp from skillet and set aside.
4. Add white wine, Parmesan cheese, lemon juice, red pepper flakes, salt, and pepper to the skillet. Cook for 2 minutes.
5. In a bowl, combine the cooked pasta, shrimp, and sauce. Transfer to a greased casserole dish and top with fresh parsley.
6. Bake for 20 minutes, until bubbly.
7. Serve hot.

Chicken and Pesto Pasta Bake

Ingredients:

- **2 cups cooked chicken**, shredded
- **2 cups cooked pasta**
- **1/2 cup pesto sauce**
- **1 cup shredded mozzarella cheese**
- **1/4 cup grated Parmesan cheese**
- **1/2 cup cherry tomatoes**, halved
- **Salt and pepper**, to taste

Instructions:

1. Preheat the oven to 350°F (175°C).
2. In a large bowl, combine shredded chicken, cooked pasta, pesto sauce, mozzarella cheese, Parmesan cheese, cherry tomatoes, salt, and pepper.
3. Transfer to a greased casserole dish and top with additional cheese if desired.
4. Bake for 20-25 minutes, until the top is golden and bubbly.
5. Serve hot.

Classic Scalloped Potatoes

Ingredients:

- **4 large russet potatoes**, peeled and sliced thinly
- **1 cup heavy cream**
- **1 cup milk**
- **2 cups shredded cheddar cheese**
- **2 tablespoons butter**
- **2 tablespoons flour**
- **1 small onion**, diced
- **1 garlic clove**, minced
- **1 teaspoon thyme**
- **Salt and pepper**, to taste

Instructions:

1. Preheat the oven to 375°F (190°C).
2. In a saucepan, melt butter over medium heat. Add diced onion and garlic, cooking until softened.
3. Stir in flour and cook for 1-2 minutes to form a roux. Gradually add milk and cream, whisking until the sauce thickens.
4. Add thyme, salt, and pepper, and stir in 1½ cups of cheddar cheese until melted.
5. In a greased casserole dish, layer sliced potatoes. Pour the sauce over each layer and repeat until all ingredients are used.
6. Top with the remaining ½ cup of cheese. Cover with foil and bake for 45 minutes.
7. Remove foil and bake for an additional 15-20 minutes, until the potatoes are tender and the top is golden brown.
8. Serve hot.

Ratatouille Casserole

Ingredients:

- **1 zucchini**, sliced
- **1 eggplant**, sliced
- **1 bell pepper**, diced
- **1 onion**, diced
- **2 tomatoes**, diced
- **2 cloves garlic**, minced
- **1 tablespoon olive oil**
- **1 teaspoon dried thyme**
- **1 teaspoon dried basil**
- **1 cup marinara sauce**
- **1 cup shredded mozzarella cheese**
- **Salt and pepper**, to taste

Instructions:

1. Preheat the oven to 375°F (190°C).
2. Heat olive oil in a skillet over medium heat. Add garlic, onion, and bell pepper, cooking until softened.
3. Add eggplant, zucchini, and tomatoes, cooking for 5-7 minutes until tender. Stir in thyme, basil, salt, and pepper.
4. Pour marinara sauce into a greased casserole dish and layer the vegetable mixture evenly on top.
5. Top with shredded mozzarella cheese and bake for 25-30 minutes, until the cheese is melted and bubbly.
6. Serve hot.

Sausage and Spinach Stuffed Shells

Ingredients:

- **12 jumbo pasta shells**, cooked
- **1 lb Italian sausage**, removed from casing
- **2 cups fresh spinach**, chopped
- **1 cup ricotta cheese**
- **1 cup shredded mozzarella cheese**
- **1/4 cup grated Parmesan cheese**
- **1 egg**
- **2 cups marinara sauce**
- **1/2 teaspoon garlic powder**
- **Salt and pepper**, to taste

Instructions:

1. Preheat the oven to 350°F (175°C).
2. In a skillet, cook the sausage over medium heat, breaking it up as it cooks. Once browned, stir in spinach and cook until wilted.
3. In a bowl, mix ricotta cheese, mozzarella cheese, Parmesan cheese, egg, garlic powder, salt, and pepper.
4. Stuff each cooked shell with the sausage and spinach mixture and place in a greased casserole dish.
5. Pour marinara sauce over the stuffed shells and top with additional mozzarella cheese.
6. Cover with foil and bake for 25 minutes. Remove the foil and bake for an additional 5-10 minutes until the cheese is bubbly and golden.
7. Serve hot.

Meatball Sub Casserole

Ingredients:

- 1 lb ground beef
- 1/2 cup breadcrumbs
- 1/4 cup grated Parmesan cheese
- 1 egg
- 2 cups marinara sauce
- 6 hoagie rolls, sliced
- 2 cups shredded mozzarella cheese
- 1 tablespoon Italian seasoning
- **Salt and pepper**, to taste

Instructions:

1. Preheat the oven to 375°F (190°C).
2. In a bowl, combine ground beef, breadcrumbs, Parmesan cheese, egg, Italian seasoning, salt, and pepper. Form into meatballs and place on a baking sheet.
3. Bake for 15-20 minutes, until cooked through.
4. In a greased casserole dish, layer the sliced hoagie rolls, marinara sauce, and cooked meatballs.
5. Top with shredded mozzarella cheese and bake for 15-20 minutes, until the cheese is melted and bubbly.
6. Serve hot.

Greek Chicken and Rice Casserole

Ingredients:

- **2 cups cooked chicken**, shredded
- **1 cup cooked rice**
- **1 can diced tomatoes**
- **1/2 cup Kalamata olives**, sliced
- **1/4 cup feta cheese**, crumbled
- **1 tablespoon olive oil**
- **1 tablespoon dried oregano**
- **1 teaspoon garlic powder**
- **1/4 cup fresh parsley**, chopped
- **Salt and pepper**, to taste

Instructions:

1. Preheat the oven to 350°F (175°C).
2. In a large bowl, combine shredded chicken, cooked rice, diced tomatoes, olives, feta cheese, olive oil, oregano, garlic powder, salt, and pepper.
3. Transfer the mixture to a greased casserole dish and top with fresh parsley.
4. Bake for 20-25 minutes, until the top is slightly golden and heated through.
5. Serve hot.

Cheesy Potato and Bacon Casserole

Ingredients:

- **4 large potatoes**, peeled and cubed
- **6 slices bacon**, cooked and crumbled
- **2 cups shredded cheddar cheese**
- **1 cup sour cream**
- **1/2 cup milk**
- **2 tablespoons butter**
- **1 teaspoon garlic powder**
- **Salt and pepper**, to taste

Instructions:

1. Preheat the oven to 375°F (190°C).
2. Boil the potatoes in salted water until tender, about 10-15 minutes. Drain and mash with butter, garlic powder, salt, and pepper.
3. Stir in sour cream, milk, crumbled bacon, and half of the shredded cheese.
4. Transfer the mixture to a greased casserole dish and top with the remaining cheese.
5. Bake for 20-25 minutes, until the top is golden and bubbly.
6. Serve hot.

Buffalo Chicken Casserole

Ingredients:

- **2 cups cooked chicken**, shredded
- **1/2 cup buffalo sauce**
- **1 cup cooked pasta**
- **1 cup shredded cheddar cheese**
- **1/2 cup ranch dressing**
- **1/4 cup blue cheese crumbles**
- **1/2 cup celery**, chopped
- **Salt and pepper**, to taste

Instructions:

1. Preheat the oven to 350°F (175°C).
2. In a large bowl, mix shredded chicken, buffalo sauce, cooked pasta, cheddar cheese, ranch dressing, blue cheese, and celery.
3. Transfer the mixture to a greased casserole dish and top with additional cheddar cheese.
4. Bake for 20-25 minutes, until the cheese is melted and bubbly.
5. Serve hot.

Lemon and Herb Chicken Casserole

Ingredients:

- **2 cups cooked chicken**, shredded
- **1 cup cooked rice**
- **1/2 cup chicken broth**
- **1/2 cup sour cream**
- **1 tablespoon lemon zest**
- **1 tablespoon lemon juice**
- **2 teaspoons dried thyme**
- **2 teaspoons dried rosemary**
- **1 cup shredded mozzarella cheese**
- **Salt and pepper**, to taste

Instructions:

1. Preheat the oven to 350°F (175°C).
2. In a large bowl, combine shredded chicken, cooked rice, chicken broth, sour cream, lemon zest, lemon juice, thyme, rosemary, salt, and pepper.
3. Transfer the mixture to a greased casserole dish and top with shredded mozzarella cheese.
4. Bake for 20-25 minutes, until the top is golden and bubbly.
5. Serve hot.

Baked Spaghetti Carbonara

Ingredients:

- **8 oz spaghetti**, cooked
- **1/2 lb bacon**, cooked and crumbled
- **3 large eggs**
- **1/2 cup heavy cream**
- **1 cup grated Parmesan cheese**
- **1/2 cup shredded mozzarella cheese**
- **2 cloves garlic**, minced
- **Salt and pepper**, to taste

Instructions:

1. Preheat the oven to 350°F (175°C).
2. In a bowl, whisk together eggs, heavy cream, Parmesan cheese, garlic, salt, and pepper.
3. In a greased casserole dish, layer cooked spaghetti, crumbled bacon, and pour the egg mixture on top. Mix well to coat evenly.
4. Top with shredded mozzarella cheese and bake for 20-25 minutes, until the cheese is melted and bubbly.
5. Serve hot.

Cranberry and Walnut Stuffing Casserole

Ingredients:

- **4 cups cubed bread** (day-old, preferably white or whole wheat)
- **1/2 cup dried cranberries**
- **1/2 cup walnuts**, chopped
- **1/2 cup celery**, diced
- **1 small onion**, diced
- **1/2 teaspoon dried sage**
- **1/2 teaspoon dried thyme**
- **2 cups chicken broth**
- **1/4 cup butter**, melted
- **1 egg**, beaten
- **Salt and pepper**, to taste

Instructions:

1. Preheat the oven to 350°F (175°C).
2. In a skillet, melt butter and sauté celery and onion until softened. Add sage, thyme, salt, and pepper.
3. In a large bowl, combine bread cubes, cranberries, walnuts, and the cooked vegetables. Add the beaten egg, chicken broth, and mix well.
4. Transfer the mixture to a greased casserole dish and bake for 30-35 minutes, until the top is golden and crispy.
5. Serve hot.

Roasted Cauliflower and Cheese Casserole

Ingredients:

- **1 medium head of cauliflower**, cut into florets
- 1 tablespoon olive oil
- 1 cup shredded cheddar cheese
- 1/2 cup grated Parmesan cheese
- 1/2 cup heavy cream
- 1/2 cup milk
- 2 tablespoons flour
- 1 tablespoon butter
- 1 teaspoon garlic powder
- **Salt and pepper**, to taste

Instructions:

1. Preheat the oven to 375°F (190°C).
2. Toss cauliflower florets in olive oil, salt, and pepper. Roast for 20-25 minutes until tender and golden.
3. In a saucepan, melt butter and whisk in flour to form a roux. Gradually add milk and cream, stirring until the sauce thickens.
4. Stir in cheddar cheese, Parmesan, garlic powder, salt, and pepper. Once the sauce is smooth, pour over the roasted cauliflower.
5. Transfer to a greased casserole dish and bake for 15-20 minutes, until bubbly and golden.
6. Serve hot.

Beef and Potato Hash Casserole

Ingredients:

- **1 lb ground beef**
- **3 medium potatoes**, peeled and cubed
- **1/2 onion**, diced
- **1 cup shredded cheddar cheese**
- **1/2 cup beef broth**
- **1 teaspoon garlic powder**
- **1 teaspoon smoked paprika**
- **Salt and pepper**, to taste

Instructions:

1. Preheat the oven to 350°F (175°C).
2. In a skillet, cook ground beef and diced onion until browned. Drain excess fat.
3. In a separate pan, cook cubed potatoes in boiling salted water until tender, about 10-15 minutes. Drain.
4. In a greased casserole dish, combine cooked beef, potatoes, garlic powder, smoked paprika, beef broth, salt, and pepper. Mix well.
5. Top with shredded cheddar cheese and bake for 20-25 minutes, until the cheese is melted and bubbly.
6. Serve hot.

Chicken and Bacon Ranch Pasta Casserole

Ingredients:

- **8 oz penne pasta**, cooked
- **2 cups cooked chicken**, shredded
- **1/2 lb bacon**, cooked and crumbled
- **1 packet ranch seasoning mix**
- **1 cup ranch dressing**
- **1 cup shredded mozzarella cheese**
- **1/2 cup shredded cheddar cheese**
- **1/4 cup green onions**, chopped
- **Salt and pepper**, to taste

Instructions:

1. Preheat the oven to 350°F (175°C).
2. In a large bowl, combine cooked pasta, shredded chicken, crumbled bacon, ranch seasoning mix, and ranch dressing.
3. Transfer the mixture to a greased casserole dish and top with mozzarella and cheddar cheese.
4. Bake for 20-25 minutes, until the cheese is melted and bubbly.
5. Sprinkle chopped green onions on top and serve hot.

www.ingramcontent.com/pod-product-compliance
Lightning Source LLC
LaVergne TN
LVHW081459060526
838201LV00056BA/2828